Moving toward the Other

Nicholas Halius, *Visitation*. Troyes, France.
Photograph by Ann Perrin, C.N.D.

Moving toward the Other: The Spirituality of Visitation

Mary Anne Foley

Congregation de Notre Dame
Wilton CT 06897

Cover art: *Visitation*, by Mary Southard, CSJ, Congregation of St. Joseph of LaGrange. Courtesy of www.marysouthardart.org

Grateful acknowledgment is also made for permission to use the following copyrighted material:

"The Visitation Journey" from *The Selected Poetry of Jessica Powers*, published by ICS Publications, Washington, D.C. By permission of Carmelite Monastery, Pewaukee, WI.

Excerpt from "On the Rainy River," from *The Things They Carried* by Tim O'Brien. Copyright © 1990 by Tim O'Brien. Reprinted by permission of Houghton Mifflin Harcourt Publishing Company. All rights reserved.

Unless otherwise indicated, scripture texts in this work are taken from the *New American Bible with Revised New Testament and Revised Psalms* © 1991, 1986, 1970 Confraternity of Christian Doctrine, Washington, D.C.

ISBN Number: 978-1-4276-4203-5
Printed in the United States of America

First Printing

Like Mary, who went in Visitation,

may our journeys be missions of praise.

Kathleen P. Deignan, C.N.D.[1]

Contents

beginning the conversation . . .

A six-month stay in France in 1990 gave me the delightful opportunity to visit many churches, from tiny chapels to magnificent cathedrals. Wherever I went, I found myself drawn to images of two pregnant women reaching out to one another, and those images were everywhere—in stone, paint, wood, glass, clay. To see my photographs, you would think that French religious art over the centuries portrayed almost nothing else!

The story depicted in those images is known as Visitation, the encounter of Mary and her relative Elizabeth, soon to become the mothers of Jesus and John the Baptist. For the members of my spiritual family, the Congregation of Notre Dame of Montreal, that story has become a way of life.

In recent years women and men—and even some children—have joined us as associates. They, too, have made Visitation their story, helping the sisters to realize more deeply the treasure it is for the Congregation, and challenging all of us to share it more widely. This little book is one response to that challenge.

For well over 1500 years, many Christians have treated Mary as an other-worldly object of devotion, from whom they begged spiritual and often material favors. In reaction, both historically and at present, others have shied away from any reference to one who seemed to be largely the pious relic of an unenlightened age. This book is written for those willing to consider a third alternative: a Mary who is companion and mentor on their spiritual journey.

Many today seek to remain spiritually grounded and responsive to the needs around them, in the midst of lives very much on-the-go. For them, Mary's Visitation with Elizabeth can illuminate what has traditionally been called contemplation in action in ways that are not apparent in images like Ignatius of Loyola's soldier enlisting in the army of Christ the King. Yet, although the outlines of a Visitation spirituality were suggested as early as the seventeenth century, the potential of such a spirituality has seldom been explored.

One person who did so was Marguerite Bourgeoys, founder of the Congregation of Notre Dame. The first part of this book presents the way she contemplated Mary's Visitation and suggests a method by which we, in a very different time, can let that same story surprise, move and inspire us, as well. Part Two examines the dynamics of each of the three "movements" of Visitation and the connections between them. In the third part we'll consider how that dynamic may be played out in concrete situations.

Conversation is at the heart of Visitation and of this book, though I'll be doing most of the talking. It has grown out of many conversations in classrooms and gatherings for prayer and reflection, on buses, at the beach. A number of these "conversations"—some without words—have inspired the little vignettes that appear in these pages; I hope they will help readers, as they've helped me, to understand Visitation and recognize it in their experience. I've also drawn into the conversation several authors whose writings explore in some way the dynamics of Visitation. The notes at the end make it possible to continue the dialogue with them.

It could be appropriate for the author of this work to be identified simply as "a sister of the Congregation," as used to be the custom for books written by members of women's religious communities. All that is written here comes out of my life within the Congregation, and so much of what is said was first suggested to me in community encounters, presentations and celebrations—and even more by the lives of its sisters and associates. In particular, Congregation sisters Lorraine Caza's theological insight, Kathleen Deignan's music, and Ann Perrin's companionship have helped more than I can say. I'll try to acknowledge other sources of particular insights where I can, but must count on the generous understanding of those who go unmentioned.

In the end, though, this is my "take" on the Congregation's tradition of Visitation spirituality, born of my experience as a well-educated white woman from the northeastern United States; it is in no way an official version. Hopefully, the book will prompt others with different experiences, especially some associates from around the world, to share how Visitation spirituality has taken shape in their lives.

I'm grateful to the University of Scranton for sabbatical time and the use of their beautiful retreat center, both of which helped this book come to birth. My hope is that this "conversation" will help you to name your own experience of Visitation and continue the conversation by your own life, in dialogue with many Elizabeths.

Approaching the Story

During those days Mary set out and traveled to the hill country in haste to a town of Judah, where she entered the house of Zechariah and greeted Elizabeth.

When Elizabeth heard Mary's greeting, the infant leaped in her womb, and Elizabeth, filled with the holy Spirit, cried out in a loud voice and said, "Most blessed are you among women, and blessed is the fruit of your womb. ..."

And Mary said: "My soul proclaims the greatness of the Lord; my spirit rejoices in God my savior. ..."

Mary remained with her about three months and then returned to her home.

Luke 1: 39-56

Chapter 1

Visitation as Icon

Miraculous events fill the first two chapters of the gospel according to Luke: an angelic messenger appears, revealing promises of God's bold and unexpected action, and then the impossible births of John and Jesus, the latter accompanied by a heavenly chorus. In between, in verses 39-56 of the first chapter, an encounter between the two mothers and a song of thanks and celebration. No angels, no apparent miracles.

Small wonder, then, that some have considered these verses merely a literary device by which Luke tied together his accounts of the two announcements and the two births. Indeed, the meeting of the women seems incidental, an interlude between the main events, almost a distraction. Perhaps as a result, in contrast to the rest of the two chapters, most of this passage has received little commentary throughout Christian history.

During the Middle Ages popular interest in the family of Jesus grew, and with it more consideration of the Visitation story. When the rosary was first established as a form of prayer in the twelfth century, the Visitation was considered one of the joyful mysteries, and a feast day began to be celebrated in various locations. Although that feast was proposed to the universal church in the seventeenth century, it did not hold a prominent place in liturgical or devotional practice, especially when compared to the Annunciation.

Francis de Sales suggested the name of Visitation for the order he co-founded with Jeanne de Chantal, precisely because it was not a major feast. Since the beginning of the order, sisters renewed their vows not on that day, but on the feast of the Presentation.

Visitation, then, would seem an unlikely source for a vibrant spirituality. Yet when Marguerite Bourgeoys founded a community of sisters dedicated to education a few decades after the Visitation Order began, she turned almost instinctively to the Visitation story as inspiration for her Congregation of Notre Dame. That feast continues to be the day sisters and associates renew their commitment through and to the Congregation.

A 17th-century guide[2]

In her writings, Marguerite Bourgeoys traces her spiritual journey and, in fact, the origins of the Congregation back to the moment when, at the age of twenty, she felt a "touch" from God as she looked at a statue of Mary. From that time, she searched for a way to live always in the presence of God, giving herself in love.

Catholic tradition suggested that women could best live such a God-centered life without distraction within the walls of a cloister. As a result, like so many devout French women of her day Marguerite applied to join the Carmelites and then another cloistered community, but both refused her. After the failure of a small experimental community in her native Troyes in western France, she became a lay associate of the cloistered Congregation of Notre Dame in that city until she was invited to become part of another experiment, the creation of the City of Mary, Ville-Marie (now Montreal) in New France.

Because that little settlement could not afford to support a cloister of religious women, Marguerite went alone but was soon joined by companions who supported themselves in various ways so that they could teach the children—French and some native children—without charge. The fact that they didn't remain within a cloister enabled these "secular sisters of the Congregation of Notre Dame" to participate fully in the life of Ville-Marie; indeed, many of them went "on mission," two-by-two, well beyond that city, to settlements all along the St. Lawrence River as far as the city of Quebec.

However, the first two bishops of New France considered their lifestyle too precarious and ordered them to be incorporated into the cloistered Ursulines of Quebec. The Congregation sisters insisted on retaining their uncloistered status, justifying it by claiming that they were called to imitate Mary when she went to visit Elizabeth.

Mary's "vie voyagère"

In her argument supporting the sisters' case, Marguerite Bourgeoys explained that according to her former spiritual adviser, there are three states of religious life for women, each illustrated by a New Testament woman. In the tenth chapter of Luke's gospel, the first two women appear in their home, Martha busy with preparations for guests and her sister Mary sitting as a disciple at Jesus' feet. Martha and Mary of Bethany provided the models for two kinds of cloistered sisters, according to this theory: those who care for the sick and those primarily dedicated to contemplation.

But the gospels reveal a different path in presenting Mary of Nazareth. Almost always she is away from home—in a stable, at a wedding feast, outside a house where Jesus is preaching, in Jerusalem and on a hillside outside the city as her son is dying. Often she is literally on the road—to and from Jerusalem, to Bethlehem and Egypt, to Elizabeth's home. Women had not yet found a way to imitate this *vie voyagère* of Mary, Marguerite was told; she and her sisters proposed to do just that.

The phrase *vie voyagère* literally means journeying life, life on-the-road; Marguerite's contemporaries often used it to describe the three years of Jesus' public life and ministry. For them, it had the connotation of "ordinary" (rather like our term "pedestrian"), and they tended to pass over this aspect of Jesus' life in order to concentrate on his eternal union with the Godhead. To speak of Mary's "journeying life" would have seemed odd, at best, and it may remain so for those who have been exposed to Marian art that almost always shows her at rest.

For Marguerite Bourgeoys, however, it made perfect sense. As she moved into the New World, she found herself forced to improvise a new way of living without the support of tradition or benefactors. Having the journeying Mary as her inspiration enabled her to cross the Atlantic seven times, once as the only woman on a ship filled with new recruits for Ville-Marie's militia. She experienced some of the peril of the *vie voyagère* one night while traveling across war-torn France by coach. To avoid the advances of some drunken guests, she had to barricade herself in one tiny room of an inn.

In Ville-Marie the colonists named her "Mother of the Colony" in gratitude for her service as godmother to their children, witness to their marriages, mourner at their funerals. She went to court with a woman accused of murdering her child and, to the sisters' displeasure, moved out of their house in order to stay with the women sent from France to marry the soldiers. Soon after her arrival at Ville-Marie, she climbed Mount Royal with a small contingent to replace the cross that symbolized their hope for the settlement. Much later she and the other sisters helped to build—quite literally—Bon Secours church. *Vie voyagère*, indeed.

The Congregation sisters translated Mary's *vie voyagère* into their lives in less striking ways, especially as they grew in number, established little schools, and made some concessions to the bishop's understanding of proper religious decorum and practice. Less than two years before Marguerite's death, they and the bishop finally agreed on rules that left them free to go where the need was, in imitation of Mary. Together with Marguerite, they chose Mary as their "mother and foundress."

In what she wrote for the Congregation, Marguerite Bourgeoys makes it clear that imitating the life of Mary involves much more than going out in response to people's needs. It comes to define the sisters' way of being in the world, including their way of relating to one another and to those they serve. In one instance, after noting the sisters' tendency to give preferential treatment to the wealthy, she reminds them that Mary "received kings and shepherds with the same love" when they came to see her infant son.

With neither the time nor the inclination to present a fully developed spirituality, Marguerite simply encourages her companions to "go through [Mary's] life and stop at whatever Our Lord inspires us to do." In a particular way, because Visitation serves as a paradigm for the whole of Mary's *vie voyagère*, the Congregation has paused there often to draw inspiration.

Recently, when describing the Congregation's spirituality many sisters and associates have focused not only on Mary's Visitation to Elizabeth, but also on her presence among the apostles at Pentecost, as described in Acts 1-2. Juxtaposing these two events does help to reveal the richness of each: solitary journey with presence at the heart of the community, inspired proclamation with silent reception of the Spirit. Mary Southard's Visitation image on the front cover portrays the encounter of the two women as illuminated by Pentecost fire.

However, I believe that focusing on both Pentecost and Visitation at the same time can dilute the force of each. The whole Christian community is called to Pentecost spirituality, though each person and group within it will understand what that means and live it out somewhat differently. The Congregation's way—its gift to the Church— is reading Pentecost and all of Mary's life—as well as our own—through the lens of Visitation.

Having journeyed across the ocean in the hope of recreating the church in a new land, surely Marguerite

Bourgeoys would rejoice at how the Second Vatican Council invited the church into a new Pentecost, recognizing and celebrating that all the people of God are called to holiness. I believe that she would want her Congregation to make available what they have learned of one path to holiness: imitating Mary's *vie voyagère*, shown in her Visitation with Elizabeth.

Gazing with soft eyes

Sophisticated 21st-century readers may find it difficult to be guided by a 17th-century woman, since we are so far removed from her world-view and practice. She most likely learned about Visitation not from reading the Bible but from spiritual books, sermons and images. Not only do contemporary Christians, including Catholics, read the Bible directly, but many have learned from scripture scholars and theologians to evaluate the historical accuracy of biblical passages, recognizing the layers of tradition that underlie them and the cultural assumptions, often patriarchal, that helped form them. Marguerite's society would have had no trouble affirming with Gerard Manley Hopkins: "The world is charged with the grandeur of God," while ours finds it difficult to believe in the reality of anything we can't taste or touch or measure.

We might be inclined, then, to smile at the almost childlike way Marguerite understands Mary and seeks to imitate her life. Her spirituality may appear sentimental, even naïve. Yet it was robust enough to sustain that pioneer and practical businesswoman through many years of confusion and great suffering. Is it possible for us to touch into that source of strength?

Doing so would require what Paul Ricoeur has called "a second naïveté." Having engaged in a process of critical reasoning and analysis, one chooses to move beyond it in order to recapture a sense of wonder. You would use imagination to fill the gaps in a story, for example, rather than analyzing the reasons behind the omissions. This involves a new way of seeing, and the practice of Tai Chi offers some hints on how to go about it.

Tai Chi is often practiced outside, with eyes open, so that the one practicing can connect with the energy in nature. The way of looking requires as much attention and discipline as the body movements. Neither scrutinizing individual objects nor allowing the eyes to dart around, the ideal is to look with "soft eyes" at whatever is present, so that the gaze supports but does not disturb the movement of energy.

The striking Russian icons found more and more frequently in Western churches and homes call for much the same way of seeing. Those accustomed to religious images painted in a more realistic style are often startled by these icons, in which the eyes of the central figure demand the viewer's attention.

Icons are intended to be windows on what cannot be seen. For that to happen you need to look with "soft eyes," not letting yourself get caught on the details of the image, but allowing it to become transparent, so that you can see through it to a deeper reality. With enough practice, we become trained in how to see, or perhaps better how to gaze, not only on the icon, but on all of reality. To put it another way, the icon can become the lens through which to view the world.

My hope is to approach the Visitation narrated by Luke as an icon through which to understand not so much Mary's life as our own. I'll take his narrative at face value, leaving for another time questions of historical accuracy and editorial perspective, so that we can allow ourselves to be caught up in its dynamic.

Most of the Visitation images I've seen capture the moment when the two women first meet, but that is only one of the small events that make up Visitation. It may be most helpful to see Visitation as a dance composed of three major movements: journey, visit, and song. The following pages are an invitation to gaze with "soft eyes" on Mary as she moves through the dance of Visitation. Then, following her lead, we too may be able to join in the dance.

A word of caution, though. Gazing with soft eyes doesn't mean failing to ask the hard questions. As a matter of fact, looking in that way encourages us to take down our guard and so become vulnerable to what we see.

Hearing the Story

THE VISITATION JOURNEY

The second bead: scene of the lovely journey
of Lady Mary, on whom artists confer
a blue silk gown, a day pouring out Springtime
and birds singing and flowers bowing to her.

Rather I see a girl upon a donkey
and her/ too held by what was said / to mind
how the sky was or if the grass was growing.
I doubt the flowers, I doubt the road was kind.

"Love hurried forth to serve." I read, approvingly.
But also see, with thoughts blown past her youth
a girl riding on a jolting donkey
and riding further and further into the truth.

Jessica Powers[3]

Chapter 2

Journey

Luke's gospel begins in what Jewish tradition considers the holiest of places—the Jerusalem temple. There a holy man—a priest—prepares to burn incense at the altar of the Most High. The scene then shifts to a small town in backwoods Galilee, to a woman with no particular religious or social status.

To both the divine messenger comes, bearing the promise of a child to be born by God's power. Great prophet though Zachary the priest's son will be, Mary's child will be greater still, will be holiness itself. Mary's "yes" to the angel's invitation makes her, even more than the temple, sanctuary of the Most High God.

Setting out

If we were writing the script, we would most likely have Mary pause right here and ponder these things in her heart, as Luke says of her so often. (Shouldn't she have made at least a three-day retreat?) Instead, she responds to the angel's message by setting out for the home of Zachary and his wife Elizabeth.

The journey of a thousand miles may begin with one step, as the proverb has it, but that first step can be hard to take. I'm always comforted to remember that Marguerite Bourgeoys hesitated before agreeing to go to Ville-Marie in

the first place. I imagine her having an internal dialogue
something like this:

> *All these women longing to bring the gospel
> to the New World, and I'm the one who has
> been asked. Such an honor, such a gift, and
> all my advisers are urging me to do it. But
> I'd be alone, the only woman—what would I
> do, and what about my dream for a
> community? Isn't that what God wants?
> Was that hope a delusion?*

> *Then, quite clearly, Mary's words: "Go, I will
> not abandon you."*

The memory of hearing those words remained with
Marguerite for the rest of her life. Trusting in Mary's
promise, she left her native country to participate in building
the City of Mary in New France.

Luke's gospel implies that after the angel leaves her,
Mary experiences none of the same reluctance before setting
out in Visitation; apparently without hesitation she goes
"with haste." But I wonder. Mary is alone and pregnant, and
the journey is bound to be strenuous, winding its way up into
the hill country. Besides, there's so much for her to do to get
ready for the birth of her own child, to say nothing of her
need for time just to take it all in. The angel doesn't
command her to go, simply tells her that Elizabeth is far
advanced in her pregnancy. Why does she go, and why with
such urgency?

Some of Marguerite Bourgeoys' contemporaries
ignored that question altogether, preferring to interpret
Mary's literal journey as symbolic of her mystical path into

God. Francis de Sales did take the question seriously, but assumed that out of charity she goes to help Elizabeth with household chores. As the unknown writer in Jessica Power's poem puts it, "Love hurried forth to serve." Marguerite's interpretation was far bolder. According to Luke, the Holy Spirit fills Elizabeth at the moment of Mary's arrival. Marguerite concluded that Mary has a mission: she is sent in order to help sanctify the older woman and the unborn John, just as the members of her Congregation had been sent to the people of New France.

There may be still more reasons why Mary sets out. Hearing that Elizabeth at long last is carrying a child offers Mary a sign that she can trust in what God is doing in herself. Being with Elizabeth can reinforce that belief. And perhaps the enormity and the uncertainty of what Mary has just experienced draws her to be with the older woman in whom also God is acting. Of course, it's not necessary to choose among these reasons. As in so many of our choices, probably all these things play a role, consciously or unconsciously, in Mary's decision to set out: the desire to help Elizabeth, a call to bring God's blessing, the need for a companion with whom to share what she holds in her heart—couldn't these all join in a single impulse to set out "with haste"?

So often the purpose of a journey, to say nothing of its consequences, becomes clear only after it has been completed, sometimes long after. It's clear to us that Mary begins the movement toward Visitation because of, and as a continuation of God's visitation to her through the angel. It may not be so clear to her that in going out to Elizabeth, she is at the same time moving more deeply into God.

On the road

Travel is unsettling. Whether chosen or imposed, and whether we do it by walking, riding, or driving, there are so many things outside our control. Of course, that's always our real situation, but in familiar surroundings it's easier to hold on to the illusion of control, and many of us give up that illusion only reluctantly. No doubt that's why the main character in Anne Tyler's novel *The Accidental Tourist* writes travel guides that provide tips on how to make travel abroad feel as much as possible like relaxing in your own living room.

At the same time and perhaps for that very reason, if we can allow ourselves to relinquish control, leaving the familiar behind and taking to the road can be liberating. It gives time and space for pondering and gaining new perspective. Some time ago, when I returned to the United States after living in Japan for five years, I found the "culture shock" greater than when I'd first arrived in Tokyo. In going to the other side of the planet, I expected things to feel strange and different, but not on my return. Apparently however, my way of seeing had changed, and, like so many travelers, I no longer understood what had seemed self-evident before. A disorienting experience certainly, but ultimately liberating.

Jessica Powers recognizes that journeying to Elizabeth must have changed Mary. Imagining that she went by donkey, the poet cautions against sentimentalizing the journey: "I doubt the road was kind." Indeed not, if it led up into the hill country. Rather, she believes, traveling jolted Mary deeper into the truth of what was happening in her, as it gave her time to ponder. Far from distracting her from God's presence and action, her journey enabled Mary to experience it more deeply.

Many of Marguerite Bourgeoys' contemporaries had difficulty in recognizing that being on-the-road could have spiritual value. As a result, early in the seventeenth century when Vincent de Paul and Louise de Marillac founded the Daughters of Charity to care for the sick poor in their homes, they met considerable opposition. To assure these women that their life could be a valid path to holiness, Vincent advised them to consider the streets of the city their "cloister," or, to put it another way, to carry their "cloister" within them.

For Marguerite Bourgeoys, the example of Mary on-the-road reveals what it means to carry your cloister within you. She urges her sisters to imitate Mary in maintaining an interior solitude, remaining present to and grounded in the experience of God's grace. Because of her presence to God, as well as the presence of God made flesh in her, Mary is God's new sanctuary. That's why she can find holiness on the path to Elizabeth's house, and not just in the Jerusalem temple.

planning room

The practice of Tai Chi illustrates this dynamic well. What to the novice seems a series of positions is really continuous movement: the instant an arm or leg reaches its full extension, for example, it begins to retreat. In order to remain balanced, you begin by sinking down, bending the knees slightly, so that you're grounded in the earth, and all further movement is done from that posture. You prepare to move by shifting your weight onto one leg, so that when you move the other to step out, you won't topple over. (At least I'm told that happens with practice.)

Sister Mary Eileen Scott, CND has characterized Marguerite's spirituality as rooted in a "dynamic of the provisional." Trying to carve out a new way for women to live the gospel, in a new land, without the presence of so influential a patron as Vincent de Paul, left her little choice but to improvise. But living the dynamic of the provisional is more than a response to circumstance; it is a necessary consequence of living in imitation of the journeying Mary's life.

When you're traveling, things around you are always changing. (That's why they say that cats, who are very sensitive to their environments, hate riding in cars.) The successful traveler needs to stay poised and ready to adapt to each new situation.

> *All his life the old man has been longing for the coming of Messiah. Every night before going to sleep, he lays out his clothes on the chair and places his shoes right next to the bed. That way, if Messiah comes before morning, he can follow him immediately.*

Poised and ready—and willing to travel light. The old man in that ancient Jewish tale saw no need for baggage, but traveling without bringing a lot of what belongs to us is risky. So we tend to take our backpacks and suitcases, our preconceptions and fears.

Staying with the journey

The mobility of the Daughters of Charity or Marguerite's "secular sisters" went against 17th-century social norms; in our time it *is* the norm. Much of our lives are taken up with moving at increasing speeds, over ever-greater distances. Powerwalking, preferably with earphones that insulate us from hearing what surrounds us, has replaced simple walking.

Paradoxically, the routine form of travel for so many—commuting—is almost always tedious, but it can become frustrating enough to escalate to murderous road rage. We want to get to wherever we're going. Like the children who begin asking "Are we almost there?" almost as soon as a trip begins, we resist being on the way. All too easily the title of a book from the 1960's becomes our prayer: "Are You Running with Me, Jesus?" But we don't have time to hear the answer.

Writing this chapter has forced me to recognize that I'm closer to that mentality than I'd like to admit. My ideas about journeying weren't coming together in the way I'd hoped, and in the time I'd allotted. Frustrated, I kept looking forward to the next chapter, when I'd finally get to talk about what's really important—or so I thought. In short, I was resisting being in-process, on-the-road, not yet arrived. The problem is that the Holy One may be on the road, waiting to encounter us, as happened for the two disciples going to Emmaus in the twenty-fourth chapter of Luke's gospel. Lest we miss the opportunity for that meeting, we need to let ourselves be present to the journey as it unfolds.

That is not easy for some of us. For most of my life, I've been known for breathless arrivals at appointments because I hadn't factored in time to travel—between floors of a building, for example. A few years ago that had to change for me as the result of surgery which, for a short time, made walking difficult and very slow. I was in a building with long corridors, and I remember calculating how long it would take to get wherever I was going and deciding if I had the energy to attempt it.

Unfortunately, that new awareness didn't stay with me after I started moving faster, but these days gasoline prices are giving me another opportunity to learn.   To conserve gas I've reduced my highway driving speed to 55 m.p.h., a practice hard to sustain with cars whizzing by, to say nothing of having to factor in an extra 10 minutes an hour of travel time. But the quality of my ride has changed. I'm seeing and enjoying the scenery more as I allow myself to be on-the-way.

If we are to carry our cloister within us, we can't be "accidental tourists"; we need to find ways of centering ourselves, what the Buddhists call one-pointedness or mindfulness. This is surprisingly difficult for many of us in our fast-paced, overstimulated world. Perhaps the time has come to revive some traditional Christian ways of experiencing journey as prayer, like processions, the stations of the cross, pilgrimage.

The Zen practice of walking meditation can help us to be attentive as we move. It consists simply of walking as slowly as possible, while noting each movement: "now the edge of my heel is touching the earth, now all of my heel is in contact, now the bottom of the ball of my foot, ..." Quite a different perspective from powerwalking! Regardless of the method used, and whether or not it's possible to move physically, Visitation requires attentiveness to and on the journey.

26

The physical aspect of journey prepares for and hints at the heart of Visitation—the interior movement toward another person. Native American wisdom suggests that it is impossible to understand the other until you have "walked a mile in his moccasins." John S. Dunne calls this kind of movement "passing over." For those seeking to understand another person, culture, or religious tradition, he advises beginning by getting in touch with yourself, your story, your view of the world—sinking down into it, we might say. Then place it down gently so that you can "pass over" to the other, listening to her story and worldview, taking it on, as it were. Dunne is convinced that in the end you will return enriched to the place you began. T. S. Eliot would add that you will know the place for the first time.[4]

Bernadette Teiko Yagi, an Associate of the Congregation from Japan, describes well the relationship between the physical and interior aspects of Visitation journey, as she has witnessed them being lived out:

> The Sisters did not choose life in the cloister. Neither did they erect walls around their hearts. They chose rather to be present to the people around them and to accept whatever that presence involved.

She goes on to speak of the grounding that makes it possible to sustain a stance of Visitation: "I believe that kind of presence is possible only for people who speak to God quietly in their hearts."

Setting out on the journey of Visitation begins the process of passing over. That means that it's never a matter of being "almost there"; if we're in Visitation we're already and always "there."

Visitation[1]

Mary: *Elizabeth . . .*

Elizabeth: *Who is this coming to greet me?*
It is she whom the Lord taught to dance,
taught to sing of God's love.
With that song on her lips,
bearing the promised hope,
she comes.

Mary: *Elizabeth . . .*

Elizabeth: *Why do you come now to see me?*
You are fair, full of grace,
and the One whom you bear is the Lord.
Why this blessing to me?
I'm old, my welcome is poor—
why come to me?

Mary: *Elizabeth,*
Rise and look up: I am Mary.
I have come, as God comes,
to the ones who believe in God's love
and power when we're weak
and the joy of promise fulfilled
and still great things to come.

Mary: *Elizabeth . . .*   Elizabeth: *Mary . . .*

Come, let us sing to the Lord:

Our being proclaims your greatness, O God.
Our spirit finds joy in you.

Chapter 3

Visit

A pamphlet published by the Congregation in the 1960's expresses the meaning of religious vocation in terms of Visitation: "Because a woman came who carried Christ within her, there was a change in someone else." Indeed, Mary's Visitation does change Elizabeth, as she feels her child move, jump, dance within her.

When I was young, I thought that Elizabeth's experience of sensing her unborn child move was something extraordinary that had to be the result of God's direct action. It was somewhat disappointing to learn that pregnant women experience this often. Fortunately, I've come to understand that my initial response was quite accurate: experiencing new life stirring—whether in the womb or in the ordinariness of daily life—really is a kind of miracle, a sign that God is present and acting.

Luke interprets John's stirring in Elizabeth's womb as a sign that Elizabeth received the Holy Spirit. As a result, like the great Spirit-filled prophets of the Hebrew scriptures, she becomes the mouthpiece of the Most High, proclaiming Mary blessed, while acknowledging her own unworthiness to receive her.

It's interesting that in this part of Luke's Visitation narrative, we don't hear Mary's voice. Her greeting to Elizabeth, which causes the child to move within her, is spoken off-stage, as it were. The voice we hear is Elizabeth's; in the memorable feminist expression, Mary's coming has heard her into speech. And she continues to speak with courage and clarity. When her child is born she does not hesitate to contradict those who assume he will be named after his father: "No, his name will be John." Visitation, then, involves becoming present to others in a way that calls them forth, enabling them to claim and speak a word that is their own.

Marguerite Bourgeoys follows many interpreters over the centuries in suggesting that not only Elizabeth but also John received the Holy Spirit as a result of Mary's visit. As we have seen, Marguerite reads this quite literally into the lives of her sisters: "We go on mission to contribute to the education of children because the Blessed Virgin, when she visited Elizabeth, contributed to the sanctification of St. John the Baptist." That was motivation enough for her to cross the Atlantic and for the women in her company to give themselves over to an unproven community in what many considered a "savage" land.

Mutuality

This reading of Visitation may give the impression that God's Spirit is somehow absent until Mary arrives. But that is far from the case. God has already intervened in Elizabeth's life, enabling her to become pregnant in the first place. And this is reflected in her child's name: "John" has been interpreted to mean "God has shown favor." The real dynamic of Visitation is captured in the early Quaker greeting: may that of God in me touch and be touched by that of God in you.

> *Quiet and frail, looking quite stern, the elderly sister is sitting alone. For several months she has been writing to a young*

*woman who decided to join the
Congregation. On this bright afternoon they
meet for the first time, both faces
transformed with joy.*

Recently, Congregation sister Stacy Hanrahan has suggested that many sisters accustomed to modeling their lives on Mary are now in an "Elizabethan" period, welcoming the young Mary who frees up the life they're bearing. Gimme-A-Break, a winter- or spring-break service program for college students, has illustrated this well. During one week the volunteers live with a group of sisters, praying with them, and sharing much of their lives while serving the disadvantaged in some way. As we had hoped, the students have really enjoyed and appreciated the experience, and have provided valuable service at the same time. However, we had not anticipated how much energy and hope they would bring to the communities in which they lived.

In fact, just as in the meeting of the old sister and the young woman beginning her life in the Congregation, it often becomes difficult to say who is Mary, and who, Elizabeth. Nor is it important to do so. In their encounter both are active and both are changed, Mary as well as Elizabeth.

Luke tells us that Mary stays with Elizabeth for about three months, a long time for a visit under any circumstances. This visit can not happen unless Elizabeth makes a place to receive Mary into her home and into her heart. Because of that hospitality, Mary has plenty of time to ponder what is happening within her. Spending those precious first months of her pregnancy with Elizabeth can help her come to terms with it, as she shares her wonder and her fears. When it feels as if she must be deluded in thinking that God is working in her, she can turn and see the new life coming to birth in the older woman. In other words, surely Elizabeth "visits" Mary, as truly as the reverse. Visitation is mutual.

Visitation refused

Marguerite Bourgeoys grew up looking at the sculpture pictured opposite the title page of this book. That beautiful Visitation still stands in the Church of S. Jean across the street from where she was born in Troyes, France. The two strong burgher women—notice Elizabeth's keys!—are just at the moment of greeting each other, the moment pictured in so many Visitation images. Here, their encounter is caught in the clasp of their hands.

A close examination of the hands reveals that they have been broken and repaired, but in such a way that signs of the break are still apparent. In some sense, this is appropriate, for it reveals how fragile the point of contact can be in life, as well as in sculpture. The fact that Mary's presence evoked joy, gratitude and wonder in Elizabeth does not mean that the gesture of Visitation will always be received in that way. All too often it meets with indifference or even rejection.

How should one respond when the gesture of Visitation is refused? Luke's Visitation narrative doesn't provide a clear answer. However, the beginning of his Acts of the Apostles offers a hint in noting Mary's presence in the Christian community after Jesus' death. For the most part, those who huddle together in Jerusalem have refused her son's visitation to them: they lost hope in his message, denied knowing him, abandoned him. Yet she chooses to remain with them and pray with them that God's Spirit will come and fill them, as Elizabeth was filled. That is to say, even in the face of rejection Mary remains open to the possibility of Visitation.

In reflecting on the commandment to love the neighbor as oneself, Marguerite Bourgeoys extends it, insisting, "we must preserve the neighbor in the love he ought to have for us." This comes close to saying that we have a responsibility to be loveable so that others can fulfill their obligation of loving us! At least it suggests that we never have the luxury of claiming that a break in relationship is simply the other person's problem. Marguerite herself was called to live this out in dramatic fashion toward the end of her long life.

A Congregation sister, Marie Tardy, began receiving what many around her considered to be revelations from God. She saw Ville-Marie mired in sin, and its leaders, including Marguerite, under the control of the devil. Several Sulpician priests in Ville-Marie supported Marie in these accusations, causing deep division in the colony, as well as within the Congregation. In the end, the Sulpician superior ordered Marie and her Sulpician supporters back to France, where she died a short time later.

Marguerite was particularly vulnerable to the visionary's accusations since, as members of the same small community, they must have known one another well. The experience caused Marguerite to doubt herself and to remain in that "darkness" for several years. Yet she and the other Congregation sisters requested that Marie be permitted to return to Montreal, and they continued, even after her death, to list her name as a member of the Congregation. Apparently, none of them thought that her actions had broken the bonds they shared.

Recent events in Lancaster, Pennsylvania have offered people around the world a striking witness to the power and demands of living Visitation. "Visited" by a stranger who slaughtered several of their children and then himself, the small Amish community there spoke, through their tears, of their willingness to forgive the murderer. Some among them went to the man's home and to his funeral because they recognized that his family too must be experiencing shock and horror, and they wanted to offer them comfort. Far from "erecting walls around their hearts," they remained willing to live Visitation.

"All real living is meeting"

Jewish philosopher Martin Buber's work helps to illuminate what is at stake in moving toward the other in Visitation. He proposes that all of us relate to everything in two ways, or as Buber puts it, we speak two primary words: I-Thou and I-It. When I approach the other—whether a book, a tree, or John—as an object, an "It," I observe it from a distance and recognize it as separate from me and having its own characteristics. When I say "Thou," however, the distance between us disappears, and "Thou" fills my horizon. As a result, the "I" that is a separate entity fades.

The fact that "I" is written the same way in both phrases is somewhat misleading. In meeting a Thou, the I is transformed in a way that the I defined by a world of objects can't begin to imagine. It becomes fully alive. This leads Buber to conclude that all real living is meeting. Visitation, then, because it is centered on the encounter with a Thou, opens the possibility of really living.

John Dunne's notion of "passing over" illustrates the kind of transformation that encounter with Thou makes possible. In my World Religions classes we try—and often fail—to observe the rule not to discuss Christianity. That rule exists in order to encourage us all to immerse ourselves as much as possible in the worldviews we study, letting them speak for themselves, as it were, rather than viewing them only in terms of their similarity to or difference from Christianity. For me, this process opens me to a deeper understanding not only of those other traditions, but also of my own.

On first learning of Buber's thought, people often conclude that he proposes eliminating the I-It word as much as possible. However, developmental psychologists would be quick to point out that we can't come to a sense of personal identity unless we learn to distinguish ourselves from surrounding objects and persons. Both primary words are necessary, but I-It has a tendency to take over. Especially in cultures that emphasize the importance of the individual, it can easily become the I's dominant way of relating to the world.

Remaining in the stance of I-It makes me feel more in control, more sure of myself and everything else, whereas saying I-Thou opens me to suffering and rejection. To speak that word is to risk everything. But refusing to speak it, failing to take that risk, diminishes my life and all my relationships, and it makes Visitation impossible.

God's visitation

Christian tradition came to name the encounter of Mary and Elizabeth Visitation, but Luke uses neither that word nor even the word "visit" in narrating their meeting. Later in his second chapter, however, he does speak of a visitation. In response to the birth of John, his father Zachary celebrates what God has done in the canticle that has become known as the *Benedictus*: "Blessed be the Lord God of Israel, who has visited and brought redemption to his people."

This idea of God's visitation is a theme extending back as far as the book of Exodus, where the God of Abraham, Isaac and Jacob instructs Moses to let the Israelites know "I have visited you and seen all that the Egyptians are doing to you." (Ex 3.16)[5] At that time and at other critical moments of their history, God's visitation saves the Israelites from oppression, but their infidelity at other times causes God to visit in punishment. Whether saving or punishing, God's visitation is always an act of power. In the New Testament, the gospels as a whole can be read as witness to God's visitation in Jesus. Can the encounter of Mary and Elizabeth in all its simplicity and ordinariness be seen as an instance of God's visitation?

Mary Southard's image of the Visitation seems to suggest just that. In a calendar which featured the image, the artist described the process by which the painting emerged:

> I began painting Mary and Elizabeth coming toward each other—the joyful welcome, life, light, and energy between them; . . . Then I saw the chalice—a single chalice—radiant with the life within each of them! The painting took on a life of its own, new meaning . . . .

Martin Buber claims that I-Thou is spoken most appropriately when addressing God, and he implies that the risk and transformation involved in any I-Thou relationship, that is to say, any relationship of real love, opens us to the Eternal Thou. Jesuit paleontologist and mystic Pierre Teilhard de Chardin makes that connection more explicit: "Between those who love one another with true charity [God] appears—he is, as it were, *born*—as a substantial bond of their love."[6]

This seems to suggest that God is their very act of loving. Of course, at least since the first letter of John was written, Christians have proclaimed that God is love. In doing so, many have thought they were naming a quality of God. For Teilhard, however, love is always a verb, an action, and so the phrase really identifies the energy that is God.

To be in Visitation is to make the journey beyond our comfort zone and expectations, truly meeting the other and staying in his reality. When we allow the other to be Thou in that way, God "is, as it were, born," and we participate in the divine energy of love. This understanding adds a new dimension to the famous assertion of third-century theologian Irenaeus: the glory of God is the human person fully alive. To be fully alive, in Buber's terms, is to be transformed by relating to a Thou, and therefore to the Eternal Thou.

As we saw above, Visitation doesn't involve bringing God to a situation devoid of the divine presence. Nor does it simply remind us that God visits us. It makes God's visitation possible and tangible; it *is* God's visitation. We might say it puts "skin" on God's loving embrace.

> *Waking up suddenly in the middle of the night, the little girl cries out* for *her mother. After some time her sobs grow quiet, and her mother murmurs, "You know, God loves you very much, even more than me. Whenever you're scared, you just need to ask, and God will be right there." From within her mother's arms the little one answers, "I know God's here, but sometimes you just need skin."*

Returning home

In the first verses of his gospel, Luke promises to keep his narrative orderly. That must be why he finishes his account of Mary's visit by noting her departure before he describes the birth of Elizabeth's son John. Yet after staying with Elizabeth for three months, how could Mary not remain with her as she gives birth? Surely Mary joins Elizabeth and Zachary, as well as their neighbors and other kinfolk, in marveling at John's birth and praising the God "who has visited and wrought redemption for his people." But then she does leave. It's time to return home, take up her life with Joseph, prepare for her own child's birth.

Visits have a natural rhythm, and there comes a time to depart, though it's not always clear when that should be. I've never seen this moment of Visitation depicted in art, though I've seen it lived, over and over. Whenever Visitation is mutually given and received, it's hard to see it end. Just as when she first sets out on the journey to Elizabeth, we want to urge Mary to stay a little longer, especially since we know what faces her, what faces them both because of the destiny of their sons.

Yet If John Dunne is right, passing over into the world of another enables us to stand in our own place in a new way and to immerse ourselves in our own world more deeply. So it must be for Mary. As she returns home, she carries with her the fruit of Visitation captured in a song. Whatever sadness may accompany the moment of leaving, it is most fitting for Visitation to end in celebration.

Magnificat[1]

Our being proclaims your greatness, O God.
    Our spirit finds joy in you.

For you've looked on us in our littleness,
    now we are blessed.
And you in your strength do great things for us—
    holy your name.

Your mercy lasts from age to age
    on those who seek your love.
The ways of your power, O Holy One,
    confuse the proud of heart.

You cast the mighty from their thrones,
    raise up the little ones.
You fill the starving with good things,
    the rich go empty away.

For you've helped your servant Israel,
    remembering your love,
        as you promised to Sarah and Abraham
            and their children:
            love without end.

Our being proclaims your greatness, O God.
    Our spirit finds joy in you.

Adapted from Luke 1. 46-55

Chapter 4

Song

The third great movement of Visitation is a prayer. Luke tells us that Mary speaks the words, but the power and beauty of the prayer's poetry have led Christians throughout the ages to sing it. Surely Mary must do so as well.

Beginning in Latin with the phrase *Magnificat anima mea Dominum*—literally, my soul magnifies the Lord—the whole song has come to be known as Magnificat. In phrases that echo the Hebrew prophets and other biblical texts, the first verses proclaim the great things that the holy and merciful One has done for God's lowly servant, while the rest of the prayer celebrates how God has overturned the fortunes of the powerful, raising up those who are hungry for food and for God.

Most commentators see little connection between the hymn and its immediate context, the encounter of Mary and Elizabeth, but viewing the song and the visit together reveals deeper meanings in both.

Magnificat as private prayer

Some years ago, John Michael Talbot created a lovely musical setting for the first verses of the Magnificat. While his song serves well as a hymn of thanksgiving and a meditation on the holiness of God, it does not capture the essence of Mary's song, to my way of thinking. For one thing, it omits all the powerful reversals of the verses that follow: the proud confused, the hungry fed, the rich left out. But in addition, it feels like the singer's private communication with God.

The idea of purely private prayer would be puzzling to Mary, coming as she does out of the rich Jewish tradition of prayer to the One who promised, "You shall be my people, and I will be your God." In fact, for most Christians up to the modern era, *my* God was always *our* God. We see this most clearly when Jesus teaches his followers to pray to his *Abba* as Our, not My, Father.

In contrast, cultures that emphasize private property, the nuclear family, and the individual tend to relegate religion to the private sphere and privatize even—and perhaps especially—our relationships with God. Recapturing some of the ancient sense of solidarity in prayer may require stretching language beyond our normal usage. I tried to do this when setting the Magnificat to music, by using as a refrain "Our being proclaims your greatness, O God; our spirit finds joy in you."

It is significant that Magnificat does not follow immediately after Mary's "yes" to the angel. When told of the great grace that is hers, the overwhelming way God is acting in her, she responds by setting out to be with Elizabeth. Their encounter, their mutual visitation that becomes God's visitation, calls forth the song. It's as if Mary can't sing Magnificat until she sees Elizabeth.

Though not a private prayer, Mary's Magnificat is deeply personal, born of an intimate relationship with God. Because of this relationship she can let herself be seen by God in her lowliness and so be blessed, and she can invite others into that relationship and that prayer.

Elizabeth's song, and ours

My understanding of Magnificat first began to change when it occurred to me to ask what Elizabeth is doing while Mary sings God's praises. Luke says nothing on the subject and so gives the impression that Elizabeth is simply a silent witness to Mary's prayer. But how could that be?

Mary is singing about what Elizabeth has experienced: God's lifting up the lowly. Not only has Elizabeth seen her status as barren woman reversed, like Hannah in the book of Samuel, but she has also felt new life stir within her as God's Spirit fills her and makes her a prophet. If asked how she had the right to join in Mary's song, she'd have to respond in the words of the nineteenth-century hymn: "How can I keep from singing?" Visitation draws Elizabeth as well as Mary into Magnificat.

Mary Southard's image of Visitation found on the front cover includes a number of shadowy figures in the background who seem to be moving toward the light at the heart of Visitation. Witnessing the encounter of Mary and Elizabeth draws them, too, into Mary's song.

> *It's the feast of Mary's Immaculate Conception, and the large downtown church is packed for the evening Mass. Many in the congregation are elderly; they've come by way of the entrance that has no stairs. Others, without work or a home, are here seeking warmth, having passed a long, cold day on the streets outside. The readings and prayers stress how beautiful Mary is in God's*

*eyes, but nothing is said about the poor, worn
people who fill the church.*

I wonder if that celebration of Mary touched the hungry
hearts of those people that December evening and drew
them into Magnificat. Maybe so, but I wish someone had
reminded them that they, too, are beautiful in God's eyes;
that Mary's story is theirs because God has chosen to visit
them as well; that they too can sing her song.

At first glance, to suggest that Mary's song can be
ours seems to deny or at least diminish the uniqueness of her
graces and her role. However, Mary of the Magnificat is
always Mary of the Visitation, moving toward Elizabeth, her
presence stirring the new life already present within the
older woman. She serves as a mirror, enabling Elizabeth to
see herself as she can be. Surely Mary's greatest joy would
be to become transparent enough that Elizabeth comes to
recognize, encounter, and celebrate the Holy One who visits
her. The more deeply Magnificat is Mary's prayer, the more
deeply it becomes the prayer of Elizabeth and all those
caught up in Visitation.

We need not fear that viewing Mary in this way will
somehow reduce her importance. Concerns about this
remind me of the time many years ago when I heard Mother
Teresa of Calcutta address an audience of several hundred
sisters. Her words about the consecrated life—and even
more, her presence—moved and challenged me deeply, and I
wanted to ask her to pray with us that we learn how to live
more faithfully. Instead, we stood and applauded,
acknowledging the value of her witness. However, by
focusing on her and all she had done, we also distanced

ourselves from her and, in a sense, let ourselves off the hook when it came to the challenge of her message. I think she would have preferred praying with us.

In some ways it's easier to let Magnificat remain just Mary's song, since entering that song requires courage. We might prefer to be let off the hook.

Courage to enter the song

In Marty Haugen's song "Gather Us In," the community asks for what they need in order to worship wholeheartedly: to be awakened, nourished, taught. The second verse concludes with a surprising additional petition: "Give us the courage to enter the song."[7]

Why should it take courage to enter Magnificat? It depends on where you stand, of course. Liberation requires that we want to be freed, and the desire begins with awareness of our need. The poor have this awareness and, like Elizabeth, have everything to gain from entering Magnificat. But what about the others? The powerful might well be reluctant to enter a song that celebrates their world being turned upside-down and proclaims that they'll lose all control—be confused, pulled from their thrones, sent away empty. It would seem that they can only lose by entering the song. Is Mary's song accessible only to those without power, then?

Many students at the university where I teach travel to Latin America and Africa on service trips, and almost always they marvel at the joy and generosity of the people they meet. The students are citizens of the world's wealthiest country and its only remaining superpower, a country that prides itself on being Number One—rich, mighty, proud of heart. Yet they find themselves asking, perhaps for the first time, what those who welcomed them have found that eludes us in the midst of our strained, hectic and often unhappy lives.

That question has led some students to make changes in their lifestyles and career choices, to learn more about their government's policies and to advocate for change. Through their experiences of Visitation in such places as Ecuador and Kenya, they have found the courage to enter Mary's song. On the other hand, it would seem that the little ones, the hungry, God's servants would jump at the chance to be raised up, filled with good things, shown merciful love. Surely they wouldn't need courage to enter this song.

Or would they? The little ones get their world turned upside down, too, and that's hard on the equilibrium. To sing Magnificat they too need to let go of their old way of being in the world. Those who have entered into therapy know well that the process of transformation to new freedom takes great courage. Martin Luther King recognized that the civil rights movement alone would not liberate black Americans. He insisted, "The Negro will only be truly free when he reaches down to the inner depths of his own being and signs with the pen and ink of assertive selfhood his own emancipation proclamation."[8]

It's easy to hesitate before such a challenge, and Elizabeth hints at this attitude when she asks, who am I that the mother of my Lord should come to me? Why this blessing to me, old and poor as I am? Yet Elizabeth receives the courage to enter Mary's song by encountering Mary, who is blessed because she believes in God's promise. Because of Visitation, Elizabeth can let herself believe in God's promise to her as well. As a result, she can join Mary's Magnificat.

Liberation theologians have helped us realize that Magnificat is a revolutionary anthem, proclaiming a new world order in which the positions of those with and without power are reversed. The theory behind most revolutions is that pressure must be brought to bear on the powerful, violently if necessary, to force them to give up control, since they will never do so voluntarily. Some revolutionaries, however, like King and his mentor Mahatma Gandhi, do not accept the premise that those with power will never choose to relinquish it.   *and "Solidarity" → Poland*

Rather, Gandhi and King led campaigns of nonviolent resistance that continually pressured both their followers and their opponents to change. Richard Attenborough's film *Gandhi* shows clearly that Gandhi's pacifism was neither passive nor weak. Again and again he stood before the powerful—judges, military officers, wealthy supporters of the independence movement—as well as before the destitute. Without fear or backing down, but with simplicity and courtesy he spoke the truth, lived out the truth in a way that invited all his listeners to embrace it.

Each of those encounters was a kind of Visitation, and the campaigns of both men achieved some success. Gandhi would go so far as to say that only nonviolent campaigns can succeed in the end. Yet the gift of Visitation was often refused, with tragic, bloody results. Even then, at the cost of their lives, both Gandhi and King remained in the stance of Visitation, seeking to draw others into Magnificat.[9]

Deeply personal as it is, Magnificat will be unique for each person who enters it. At the same time, given its revolutionary nature, perhaps it's just as well that it is not simply a private prayer. All of us need to be caught up in Visitation in order to have the courage to sing it.

Living the Story

Chapter 5

Finding a Place in the Story

Most chapters of this book begin with a text to stimulate your reflection. This time there is only a blank page, an invitation to pause and allow the Visitation story to echo in your memory and your heart.

A group of CND sisters and associates used to meet once or twice a year to plan events for sharing Visitation spirituality with colleagues and friends. It usually took a while to get to the items on the agenda because we seldom saw one another and wanted to find out what was going on in everyone's life. We began to incorporate time for that kind of sharing into our meetings and gradually came to name what we shared, "Visitation stories."

Indeed, the sharing itself was Visitation. (I suppose it helped that we had to travel up into the hill country of Connecticut to attend the meetings!) Reflecting over time on the encounter of Mary and Elizabeth helped us to recognize the ways that same story was unfolding in our lives. When we're attuned to the ways Visitation is taking place in the people and situations that surround us, and in ourselves, then Visitation has become an icon through which to read the sacred scripture of our lives. It becomes our story, and recognizing that can free us so that more and more our lives become the dance of Visitation.

At the end of this book you will find several ways of reflecting on the story of Visitation, allowing it to tell itself in you. That kind of reflection has led C.N.D. sister Stacy Hanrahan to describe eight "aptitudes"—beliefs, predispositions, skills, and practices—for Visitation spirituality that provide training for that dance. Each of the aptitudes can be seen, at least implicitly, in the Visitation story as Mary and Elizabeth live it.

We've seen that in Mary's presence Elizabeth finds and speaks in her own voice. And John Dunne reminds us that "passing over" to the world of another person begins by becoming aware of, in touch with oneself. **Fidelity to self** makes possible relationships that are not only caring, but also respectful and free.

At the same time, Visitation can't happen without a **readiness to welcome the other** in his foreignness. This means attuning the ear to a different way of speaking, attuning the heart so that my outlook can be changed. Since Visitation is **mutual**, changing both Mary and Elizabeth, so the one seeking to join their dance must remain convinced that in every relationship each person has something to give, to teach, to receive from the other.

In Magnificat, Mary and Elizabeth rejoice that God has "looked on us in our littleness." This means that they have recognized their own littleness and allowed God to see and perhaps smile at it. There's a certain playfulness in Visitation that can help us **not to take ourselves too seriously**. After all, we're newcomers on the planet and so should have what Stacy calls an "appreciation for imperfection" in ourselves and others.

MUTUALITY	FIDELITY TO ONESELF	OPENNESS TO WHAT IS OTHER/ DIFFERENT/FOREIGN
SOLIDARITY	**APTITUDES** **for** **VISITATION**	COMMITMENT TO LEARNING WAYS OF NONVIOLENCE
SENSE OF HUMOR and GRATITUDE	ABILITY TO CONVERSE WITH GOD	HOPE

Developed by Stacy Hanrahan, C.N.D., 2005

Being so deeply loved, imperfections and all, draws us into **thankfulness**, sustained by the habit of **conversing with God**. Luke tells us that Mary often ponders in her heart and in God's presence all that is happening in her life. In order to follow her example, we need to learn ways to pray and contemplate, and practice them over and over again. Those practices can enable us to live in **hope**, with the courage to stand up for what is right and true and the wisdom to know when to be patient.

The late Pope John Paul II challenged participants in the first world conference of the Global Forum to advance

> a more human world for all—a world in which every individual will be able to participate in a positive and fruitful way, and in which the wealth of some will no longer be an obstacle to the development of others, but a help.[10]

A world, in other words, in which everyone can sing, "Magnificat!"

Especially in light of today's increasing globalization, John Paul goes on to explain, moving toward such a world demands the virtue of **solidarity**, a deeply rooted solidarity with all those who are poor, oppressed, excluded. Living out the "passing over" at the heart of Visitation leads to that sort of solidarity, which moves us to change the systems that maintain poverty.

The virtue of solidarity can take root only in hearts that are disarmed, that is, hearts converted to **nonviolence**. As our discussion of Gandhi and King made clear, the way of nonviolence is a demanding one that may cost, in Dietrich Bonhoeffer's phrase, no less than everything. For most of us, learning to walk that path is a slow process that begins with changes in practice leading to new patterns of behavior and thought. Among the practices Stacy notes are cordiality, civility, kindness, truthfulness, forgiveness, mindfulness.

Anyone who hopes to become adept at the dance of Visitation must cultivate all of these "aptitudes," but most of us find that we move quite awkwardly in at least some of them. So it's important when contemplating our efforts to live Visitation that we continue to gaze with soft eyes, practicing toward ourselves the nonviolence we try to practice toward others.

The next two chapters will sketch out ways in which the dance of Visitation can shape all our interactions, especially those by which we seek to serve others.

His commanding officer orders the soldier to eliminate his enemy. A few days later, on finding the soldier chatting with the man he has been ordered to kill, the officer erupts in anger. This confuses the soldier, who responds, "But I did what you asked: I did get rid of my enemy—by making him my friend."

Chapter 6

Conversation as Spiritual Practice

At the most basic level, Visitation is a conversation that becomes a song of the Spirit. Yet all too often our conversations seem accompanied by a very different tune.

> *The meeting was long and contentious, and in the end they couldn't come to any agreement. Finally it's over and she just wants to escape. Then she hears about this chapter: "You're writing about the spiritual value of conversation? You've got to be kidding!"*

Indeed, my meeting-weary friend has good reason for her skepticism about living Visitation in most of our encounters. Despite the time, creativity, energy and money that modern industrialized Western societies have invested in communications, we seem to have lost the art of real conversation.

Cellphones and talk shows

In spite of the frantic pace at which we live, Americans want to be accessible at all times and places. Memories of those on the hijacked planes and in the doomed buildings on September 11, 2001 have convinced many that cellphones provide that accessibility, but at considerable cost. More and more often, in a group of people—even a group of two—at least one person interacts not with those physically present, but with unseen partners on the phone.

This reminds me of the "parallel play" of very small children. Even when they're in the same place and engaging in the same activity, each child tends to play independently, because he hasn't yet developed the social skills to interact effectively with others. The fact that cellphone users' attention is often diverted to another simultaneous activity— driving a car, working on a computer, cooking—further calls into question the quality of these phone interactions.

To those of other cultures, Americans often give the impression of being always available, as evidenced by offices where all the doors either remain open or have been eliminated altogether. Yet it's impossible to sustain such constant availability: people find more subtle ways of protecting themselves from intrusion.

In comparison to North Americans, people in Japan tend to preserve more "personal space" in their daily interactions. The crammed commuter trains going into their cities daily make this physically impossible, but many people create a virtual personal space by eliminating communication on the trains—no eye contact, no change in facial expression, no conversation.

Americans usually protect themselves differently, by talking more, not less. Hence the popularity of call-in radio talk shows. Ordinarily, the host begins by expounding on the issue of the day, often at such length that few callers have the chance to speak. She then listens just long enough to see if the callers agree with what she has said; if so, they are

58

hurried off the air. The "host" takes more time with callers who disagree, since they provide the opportunity for witty putdowns.

In addition to demeaning those who disagree, such shows reduce the complexity of profound issues to two opposing viewpoints. This reinforces the message we receive again and again, in religious as well as political circles, that all of us must take one of two positions on all major political and personal issues, as if we were choosing up sides in an elementary school game, or declaring what team we support for the World Series. Are you conservative or progressive, pro-life or pro-choice? Do you support international cooperation or national security, tolerance or family values? Do you believe in religion or spirituality, in humanity or God?

Is it any wonder that attempts at conversation so often result in impasse, shedding heat rather than light? Even when the tone remains polite, all too often there comes a point when speech becomes clipped, eyes narrow, faces harden. In the midst of strong disagreement, I've seen a look of disdain on the faces of people I greatly admire, and I fear that people have seen the same on mine.

Breakdown in communication on the interpersonal level has serious implications in societies where weapons are easily available. Historically it lies at the root of much global conflict as well, and in the last century we have acquired the technical ability to destroy the planet in the course of such conflict. Learning or relearning the art of conversation is not simply desirable for our world; it may be necessary for survival.

Visitation can initiate us into the art of conversation, but only if we allow ourselves to undergo a change of heart. The good news is that Visitation has been known to happen even on cellphones!

Conversion and passing over

To make sense of the idea that conversation requires a change of heart—that is, a conversion—it helps to note that both words are related to the Latin words for "together" and "to turn." Over time "conversation" evolved in meaning: turning to the other → intimate expression, sexual or otherwise → intimate verbal expression → any direct verbal exchange. Those who hope to retrieve the possibility of conversation today would do well to recognize some of the rich connotations of the word; it implies not only speaking words but turning toward, attentiveness to, and intimate association with someone else.

If I am turned in on myself, it's literally impossible to be turned toward the other. Real conversation, then, involves turning away from preoccupation with self. Many religious traditions identify the change of heart that enables someone to move beyond self as the first step on the journey toward God. It's also the first step toward becoming fully human. When such a conversion does not occur, conversations come to resemble parallel monologues, in which the participants do not listen to one another, but rather use the time the other is speaking to prepare what they will say next.

Conversations that become Visitation move beyond simply turning toward the other; they invite us to "pass over" to the other person's reality, in John Dunne's phrase. As we *Keep an open mind while listening* have seen, this implies letting go of preconceptions and prejudices enough to be able to enter the thought-world of the other before returning "home." Between those willing to embark on the journey of passing over, conversation moves back and forth with an ebb and flow that changes both.

Recently I learned something of that kind of passing over in a training workshop in nonviolence, sponsored by the Fellowship of Reconciliation:

> *Eight of us stand in a circle, before each a card describing someone whose circumstances and viewpoint are different from our own. A few moments to get in touch with what it feels like to be that person. Turning back into the circle, one by one we react to a particular scenario as if we were the person on our card. A pause to let what we have heard sink in. Then we each step to the left, to a different card, and "become" someone new. Eight times in all, forming the circle of truth.*

Perhaps the most important element of the Circle of Truth exercise is the pause before turning into the circle and speaking. At the outset, our facilitators cautioned us against falling into clichés when representing the position of the person on our card; they advised us to use that brief pause to connect with the person's fears and concerns, hopes and dreams, and then to speak out of that awareness.

The scenario we discussed was one about which all of us had strong opinions, and probably no one's opinion changed as a result of the exercise. We did return to the place from which we had started, as Dunne promises. But to the extent that we were able to pass over into the perspective of the eight people we "became," something did shift for us. Now, when we hear people speak from one of those perspectives, it's more possible really to hear them and perhaps to respond in a different way.

Hearing one another into speech

In Visitation conversation, silence plays a significant role. In his *Rule for Monks* Benedict of Nursia orders that at community meetings everyone be given the opportunity to speak, in order to ensure that the Spirit's voice will be heard. After all, the monks couldn't know beforehand through whom the Spirit would speak. Practically speaking, if all are to speak the leaders must choose to be silent, at least for a time. Marguerite Bourgeoys seems to share Benedict's concern when she urges her sisters to be silent so that a child may speak.

Tim O'Brien's fictional memoir of the Viet Nam war, *The Things They Carried*, illustrates powerfully the importance of silence. In the fourth chapter, the narrator becomes distraught after receiving a draft notice and runs off to the inappropriately named Tip Top Lodge in Minnesota, close to the Canadian border. For six days he wrestles with the idea of crossing the border to avoid induction, and Elroy, the proprietor, silently witnesses his struggle. Tim later recalls how Elroy was present to him during those days:

> What I remember more than anything is the man's willful, almost ferocious silence. In all that time together, all those hours, he never asked the obvious questions: Why

was I there? Why alone? Why so preoccupied? If Elroy was curious about any of this, he was careful never to put it into words.

. . . One thing for certain, he knew I was in desperate trouble. And he knew I couldn't talk about it. The wrong word—or even the right word—and I would have disappeared. . . . The man's self control was amazing. He never pried. He never put me in a position that required lies or denials. . . . Simple politeness was part of it. But even more than that, I think the man understood that words were insufficient. The problem had gone beyond discussion.[11]

In the end, without ever saying a word on the subject, Elroy enables his guest to make a choice.

As children many of us were taught not to interrupt when someone else is speaking, a principle of etiquette that seems less and less the norm. Important though that principle may be, the kind of silence that leads to passing over goes far beyond not speaking. It calls for an inner silence, becoming aware of whatever mental "static" is making it hard to hear. Sometimes just acknowledging the static to myself or even to my conversation partner creates enough space that I can begin to hear.

Hearing another person into speech demands intent listening, the way we have to listen to someone speak a foreign language, or even someone who speaks our own language, but with a foreign accent. Not long ago I participated in a five-day gathering of over three hundred

an inner certitude

Congregation sisters and associates who spoke four languages. We met several times in three different groups of eight, two of which involved at least two languages. Some in these groups knew more than one of the languages, but there were no professional translators. Yet somehow we managed to hear and understand one another, and that experience seemed to prepare us for when we met in single-language small groups, where we continued to speak simply and listen intently, and as a result shared very deeply.

In conversation people often say, "I know just what you mean" in order to encourage the one who has been speaking. The phrase seems to suggest that I've heard you and understood. But in reality we often begin as "foreigners" to one another. When we begin to speak, I probably don't know what you mean, but if I can wait and listen, our conversation may give you the opportunity to reveal it to me.

> *A young sister who lives in a large community has decided to leave religious life and wants to tell each community member herself. Worried about the reaction of some older sisters, she begins by approaching her friends, one by one.*
>
> *After several days, she takes stock, bracing herself for the more difficult conversations to come. To her surprise, she finds that there's no one left to tell. She has spoken to everyone in the house, and they all have received her lovingly and encouraged her in what she is about to do.*

Apparently, each of her conversation partners really heard her, and this enabled her to speak in the next conversation in such a way that the person she met could hear and accept her, as well.

The process of hearing one another into speech can play a significant role not only between individual persons, but also within groups. Of late, many groups have chosen to make decisions by consensus rather than executive decree, and this requires multiple meetings. Some have suggested that attending such meetings may be the asceticism of the modern age. I think I might prefer to wear a hairshirt!

For me, one of the most difficult aspects of living in Japan was the seemingly endless meetings. One faculty meeting on a rather delicate topic lasted over two hours—and even I knew before it started what the outcome had to be. A great opportunity to practice asceticism, no doubt, but to my Western sensibilities a huge waste of time.

That evaluation rested on my assumption that meetings take place in order to weigh evidence and so come to decisions. Eventually, I came to understand that the intent of gatherings like that faculty meeting is rather to give everyone who has a perspective on the issue a chance to speak and be heard. In this way everyone can become more comfortable with the decisions that, in the end, must be made.

Those of us anxious to "call the question" at a meeting, take a vote and then be on our way, have much to learn from this approach. Frequently, our way of proceeding leaves a significant number of people feeling that they have been left out of the process, and as a result they have no opportunity to "enter the song."

Making peace

I've recently learned of a mother who responded to the bullying her six-year-old son was receiving from a classmate by taking a few minutes at the bus stop each morning to greet that child, speak about what he would do that day, and wish him well. Over time the child's behavior has changed, so much so that he and her son have become friends. But the mother has changed as well, warming to the child and beginning to look out for his needs.

Though I know almost nothing about firearms, the dictum that you can't shoot someone while you're talking to him makes sense to me. However, the Muslim tale of peacemaking that precedes this chapter reveals that conversation can go much further than preventing physical violence. It can eliminate the need or even the desire to harm the other. So too, conversations in which leaders of "enemy" nations began to tell one another their hopes for their grandchildren have led to concrete proposals for reduced hostilities and even cooperation.

Of course, it doesn't always work out that way; sometimes the exchange isn't mutual, and sometimes the other can't or won't listen, and attacks instead. Nations usually respond to such provocation by breaking diplomatic relations with, if not directly counter-attacking, the offending party. Individuals, too, often end all conversation at that point, sometimes for years, presumably as a way to punish the other as well as protecting themselves from further offense.

Ironically, however, breaking off conversation makes a positive resolution less likely and thus punishes everyone, including oneself. So often conflict results from a failure to really hear one another in the first place. Continuing to speak, and even more to listen, makes it possible to find a way out of the conflict. Entering into and sustaining conversation even in the face of opposition is an exercise in the nonviolence that leads to peace. It requires courage and the willingness to suffer and to wait . . . as a woman must wait until her child is ready to come forth.

John Dear believes that the Visitation illustrates the nonviolence in action to which all Christians are called, and he identifies Mary and Elizabeth's nonviolent action as "spiritual conversation." Indeed, their conversation is explicitly spiritual, but not everyone is ready to enter into that level of conversation. As the nervous draftee at Tip Top Lodge recognized, words can frighten people away—even the "right" words, and, we might add, particularly God-words. Yet, as our reflection on the dynamic of "visit" revealed, even when God's name is not spoken, Visitation can happen in any genuine I-Thou encounter: God can be "born" without being named.

While Visitation conversation may not be explicitly spiritual, especially at first, it always draws those who experience it toward Magnificat, toward thanksgiving and praise and rejoicing in the upside-down world of the One who is love, who is peace. Dear is quite right about the goal of Visitation: to become "not only each other's friends, but friends of God, members of God's community," what Martin Luther King calls "the beloved community." This community begins in conversation.[12]

For we are [God's] handiwork,
created in Christ Jesus
for good works
that God has prepared in advance,
that we should live in them.

Eph. 2:10

Chapter 7

Serving in the Spirit of Visitation

Marguerite Bourgeoys understood her little congregation to be God's handiwork, created for the good work of building up the body of Christ in the city of Mary, Ville-Marie, following a plan that God had initiated. In this work and in the whole of their lives, Marguerite and her sisters sought to follow the way Mary lived on earth.

Their attention to Mary's activity, especially in the Visitation, challenged seventeenth-century assumptions about how women could become holy. Contemplating the holiest of women as she goes to be with Elizabeth convinced them that holiness for both women and men is not only compatible with active service, but flows into it naturally.

Service as product

Most twenty-first-century Western Christians begin with far different assumptions than those of Marguerite or her contemporaries. Thanks to modern technology, we're ever more aware of the overwhelming needs of our brothers and sisters throughout the world, and we believe that somehow we ought to respond. Furthermore, we've come to recognize that all the followers of Christ are called to lives of holiness and service. In a variety of ways, directly and indirectly, in public and in private, women as well as men are finding the means to respond to that call.

It may seem, then, that Visitation has little to offer contemporary Christians who seek a spiritual grounding for lives of service. In reality, however, it challenges some of our assumptions about service as much as it did those of our seventeenth-century ancestors.

Our culture prides itself on taking initiative, pulling ourselves up by our own bootstraps, setting and meeting goals, working efficiently. We are taught to value what we do in terms of productivity, always keeping an eye on the bottom line. It's difficult not to internalize these values and then translate them into the spiritual realm. It seems to me that too often contemporary first-world Christians evaluate themselves by their work, especially when that work provides service as a product. They—we—are tempted to get lost in the activity and ignore its Spirit-dimension, becoming enmeshed in the world of I-It.

As Martin Buber observed, we can relate to other people either as objects or as full persons by saying I-It or I-Thou. While both forms of relationship are appropriate in different circumstances, the I-It form tends to dominate because it demands far less of the "I," enabling the "I" to remain in control. So-called consumer societies, in which objects come to define human worth and even identity, can aggravate this tendency. Strange though it may seem, this can be true even for those involved in direct service.

Certainly the I-It relationship plays a vital role in effective service. In the first place, those who serve need its objectivity in order to distinguish between their own needs and those of the people they hope to serve. Really meeting others' needs demands analysis, planning and evaluation, all activities that require us to distance ourselves to some extent from the persons before us. If we allow these tasks to define our roles completely, however, then those we serve can become mere objects to us, and in the end we may lose sight of them altogether.

Visitation implies a different sort of relationship, a different stance, a different kind of productivity.

The "productivity" of Visitation

In the first movement of Visitation, as Luke recounts the story, Mary learns of Elizabeth's pregnancy from the angel who declares Mary full of grace and receives her yes to the invitation to bear God's Son. As soon as she hears about Elizabeth, Mary sets off quickly, eagerly, and apparently without a plan.

○   *rooted in grace*

Service in the spirit of Visitation flows out of the experience of being graced by God. Sometimes we simply happen into it; it does not always wait for what we consider the "right" moment, when we are prepared and everything is in place. The story is told of a professor who complained that students constantly interrupted him, distracting him from his work. One day, however, he recognized that those "distractions" were the most important aspect of his work. Living Visitation calls for a readiness to be interrupted, distracted, surprised.

Of course, service is not always spontaneous. Often we must choose and plan how we will serve, and then continue serving day after day. Even and perhaps especially then, it is important to hold our plans lightly. The initiative remains God's, and so does the "product." In the *Bhagavad-Gita*, so beloved of Hindus, the god Krishna directs his young devotee to put his whole heart and soul into what he is doing and at the same time to let go of the results, to renounce the fruit of his action.

Maintaining the delicate balance between passion for service and nonattachment to the outcome can be very difficult. In liturgical music, for example, musicians and singers offer worship communities an important service that requires considerable preparation and careful execution. But what happens when the listeners applaud? As a performer, I may want to bow, acknowledging the listeners' recognition of what we have done, or to cringe, disturbed that they haven't understood that we were trying to lead them in prayer. In either case, I remain focused on the results.

Humbling though it is to admit it, the impulse for service often comes from our need to be needed or our need to succeed. Another possible response to applause is to join in so as to celebrate, as the music does, the great things God has done—even through us who want to be recognized for our service. Acknowledging our mixed motivation can be the first step to renouncing the fruit of our action.

At the same time, the angel's message to Mary remains true of us as well: "blessed are you . . . the Lord is with you." We are God's work of art formed for the "good works" God has planned, according to the letter to the Ephesians, and we need to remain grounded in that awareness. We need to make our own the prayer of the olive tree found in an unpublished song by Evelyn Avoglia: "Let your mercy, O Lord, be the ground of my faith. Let my service have its roots, O Lord, in your kindness to me." Continuing to serve in the spirit of Visitation requires reaching down into that well of mercy and kindness again and again, praying as if everything depended on God because it does. All is grace. At the same time we must work as if it all depended on us, for in some sense that is also true.

At least it is true of the small response each of us can make to the myriad of complex needs that confront us. "We cannot do everything," as a favorite prayer of Salvadoran Archbishop Oscar Romero reminds us, because "We are workers, not master builders; ministers, not messiahs." Remembering that fact frees us for more wholehearted service, rooted in the Master Builder's merciful kindness:

> This enables us to do something,
>   and to do it very well.
> It may be incomplete,
>   but it is a beginning,
>   a step along the way,
>   an opportunity for the Lord's grace
>   to enter and do the rest.[13]

°   *a listening presence*

The second movement of Visitation begins with Mary's arrival at Elizabeth's home. In those first moments of their encounter, Mary serves Elizabeth not by what she does or says, but by her presence to the older woman and to God's action within her. This may be the most challenging aspect of Visitation service for many of us. The urgent needs of the hungry, thirsty, naked, alienated, imprisoned draw us into service, and we want to do something! It's hard to believe that our presence could be enough.

The experience of "open space" gatherings can help us learn about the importance of simple presence. It happens when the organizers of an event carve out some unstructured time, for which the first and only rule is "show up"—be there and let whatever happens, happen. No predetermined goals, objectives, or even subject matter. And in that messy process, things do happen. "Products" emerge in unexpected ways.

Letting go of structures and being willing to be surprised may work for occasional meetings, but how can it apply to daily service in structured settings and even more, to a life dedicated to service? My experience in Japan gave me some hints about how that can be. One day, a wise sister from the States who had lived in Japan for many years found me frustrated and overwhelmed at the difficulty of the language. She commented gently, "It's probably just as well that we can't speak Japanese for a long while after we arrive. If we could, we'd be sure to say the wrong thing!" Though I might not have done so voluntarily, circumstances forced me to adopt Mary's stance of listening to Elizabeth.

It's also possible to choose that posture deliberately. These days when CND sisters first go to serve in foreign settings, even when they know the language they often do not move right away into a specific work of service. Rather they are asked to take several months exercising a "ministry of presence" during which the people there can begin to reveal themselves and their giftedness, as well as their need.

It's important to maintain a "ministry of presence," making room for that listening stance, even after the initial stages are over and we're engaged in very active service. This implies a discipline of stopping at regular intervals to take stock. It also suggests that another "rule" needs to be added to the one proposed for "open space": stay long enough to listen and really hear. That may take a long time indeed.

The Nonviolent Peaceforce provides a practical illustration of the power of presence. That organization sends teams of unarmed civilians from various countries into situations of conflict, when invited by local groups. Recognizing that peace must be created by the parties to the conflict, the Peaceforce understands their role as supporting that process. They do this by accompanying individuals and groups in threatening situations, by witnessing and bringing international attention to events as they unfold, and in some cases, by "interpositioning," placing themselves physically between antagonists in situations with a potential for violence.

They also support the process of peacemaking simply by engaging in conversation. On first arriving in an area, team members visit as many local groups as possible, primarily to listen to them. Team members then sustain that conversation, continue that listening presence, over the two years of their service, often making it possible for those groups to speak to one another, as well.[14]

The need to begin from a listening stance points to another characteristic of service in the spirit of Visitation: mutuality. In order for service to become true Visitation, the one serving allows himself to receive from, as well as give to, the one being served. Not only Elizabeth, but also Mary is changed, freed by their encounter to sing Magnificat and to draw Elizabeth into her song. Both are overtaken by something greater than either of them had expected.

To emphasize the mutuality of Visitation, in this chapter I've spoken of service rather than ministry. Certainly, all Christians are "equip[ped] for the work of ministry, for building up the body of Christ" (Eph 4:12). And since the second Vatican Council, more and more Catholics have come to recognize their call to minister. Yet most people continue to associate ministry with a small number of specially designated individuals who offer a unique kind of service. It's not always clear that the "ministers" need to receive as well as give.

Visitation means serving in a way that invites everyone into Magnificat, the joyful song celebrating the One who turns everything upside-down. Sustained by that song, it becomes possible to renounce the fruit of our service and move on even before the work is complete, and we see the end results. After all, as Romero's prayer concludes, "We are prophets of a future not our own."

My years of experience as a student, teacher, and colleague have taught me a great deal about the dynamics of education in the spirit of Visitation. I share some reflections in the hope that they will help you discover how to live out Visitation in whatever forms of service you find yourself.

Liberating education

Since the time of Marguerite Bourgeoys, the Congregation has engaged in education, usually in schools. Recently, however, like other similar congregations of women, many CND sisters have begun to serve in a wide variety of venues, from retreat houses and drop-in centers to hospitals, prisons, and homes. At times, this has caused tension within the Congregation, and at a decision-making assembly several years ago, opinion was divided as to whether we should declare education a primary direction of the Congregation.

We had been studying a wide variety of social problems, noting how schools and other institutions often functioned in ways that keeps people oppressed. Someone proposed that we name what we seek to do "liberating education," in Paolo Freire's memorable phrase, and this received virtually unanimous affirmation. I can recall only a single objection: one member contended that the phrase "liberating education" is redundant, since education, as she had experienced and practiced it in the Congregation, is necessarily liberating.

Indeed, Visitation always liberates, as does educating in that spirit. This sort of education can take many forms:

- creating a school where corporal punishment may not be used in a country where that is the ordinary means of discipline
- gathering local women in a large kitchen where they can share recipes and hopes as they prepare food for a soup kitchen
- accompanying upper-middle-class teenagers on their first exposure to people in great material need, or an abused woman who must testify in court
- showing someone how to read, to speak a new language, to create beautiful music, to care for a child, to pray
- sitting with a family as their loved one passes away from them.

In whatever mode it happens, liberating education always hears the other into speech. Like Elizabeth at Mary's arrival, each of us comes to discover our own voice.

The last major assignment is to present her own model of church, and the young woman, panicked, approaches the instructor. No way will she get a good grade in the course, since class participation is factored in, and she never speaks out loud in class. Now this! She

*can't possibly create a model of church, much
less present it. Yet, as they talk, it turns out
that the student does have ideas about what
church is and could be; she even has an
image that captures those ideas.*

*Her voice, on the day of the presentation, is
strong and clear.*

Educating in a way that enables people to speak in their own voice means relinquishing some of the control often associated with the role of teacher. Henri Nouwen illustrates the way to truly liberating education when he compares the role of the educator to that of a host who welcomes guests into her home. Having taken care to arrange everything for their comfort and ease, she offers the best she has so they will be filled and then, when it's time for the guests to depart, gives them what they need for the journey and wishes them god-speed. No wonder Jesus turned so often to the image of the wedding feast to describe the new world he was inaugurating.

Nouwen's notion of hospitality is relevant whether the guests come into our office, classroom or chapel, or whether we go to their homes, hospital rooms, prison cells. Whatever the circumstances, education that liberates involves laying out and then sharing in the feast. It would never do to have the host merely sit by and observe the guests eating![14]

During the twentieth century many began questioning the degree to which traditional teacher-centered classrooms stimulated learning. In reaction, some teachers moved to a student-centered approach, giving over to the students the power to determine what they would learn and, in large measure, how they would learn it. Parker Palmer refuses to choose between those two alternatives, proposing instead a subject-centered education, in which both teacher and students remain focused on the Great Idea that occupies them. The one designated as teacher provides resources that illuminate the Great Idea and helps keep everyone focused on it. Everything culminates in a celebration of the Great Idea, a kind of Magnificat.[15]

Experiences of team teaching have helped me understand something of what Palmer means. Whether teaching American Studies with a historian, Developmental Spirituality with a psychologist, or Introductory Theology with undergraduate teaching assistants, those of us called "teachers" have delighted in becoming students as we learned from one another's perspectives. The other students often found themselves drawn into our little learning community as a result.

In such a process the lines between host and guest, server and recipient, teacher and student become blurred. At times the "student" will lead the way, if the teacher is able to let that happen.

> *Twenty-three five-year-olds flutter around their teacher, who gently quiets them so they can begin the day's program. One little girl leans over and whispers, "Can I tell you something?" The teacher stops, listens, and creates a space in which that little girl and every other child can tell one thing. Then they begin the first planned activity together quite happily.*

I suspect that teacher was as happy as her charges. In Visitation something is freed up in us by the freedom experienced by the other. A strange kind of mathematics: the opposite of a zero-sum game in which one person's gain requires that the other lose in some way. Here everybody can win.

In a surprising way Elroy, proprietor of the Tip Top Lodge, illustrates the dynamic of Visitation service. Even though, if asked, he would have muttered that he didn't do nuthin,' in reality Elroy functions as host and educator for his young friend. Having received his guest in a way that he can accept, Elroy maintains respect for him throughout their time together. The boy, now a man, recalls

> At times I felt the awkwardness of an intruder, but Elroy accepted me into his quiet routine without fuss or ceremony. He took my presence for granted, the same way he might've sheltered a stray cat—no wasted sighs or pity—and there was never any talk about it.

As has already been noted, Elroy is a man of few words. But he is a man of action, who knows that his guest requires more than shelter. When he realizes that his visitor's time with him is drawing to a close, he breaks from his ordinary routine by taking him on a fishing expedition by boat. When they come within sight of the Canadian border, he drops an anchor and waits, maintaining his silence as his guest whimpers, sobs, and finally makes his decision. As the young man understands it later, "I think he meant to bring me up against the realities, to guide me across the river and to take me to the edge and to stand a kind of vigil as I chose a life for myself."[16]

In the end, of course, the young man himself must choose, but he can do so because he has been guided and taken "to the edge," so that he could see and confront what is real. Elroy's "vigil" is a "ministry of presence" in which his willingness to wait gives the boy space—and hope. At that moment no Magnificat is possible for either of them, and the boy leaves without acknowledging Elroy's role or even revealing his decision. But as his life unfolds, the boy comes to accept the choice he has been able to make, and the novel *The Things They Carried* celebrates the life he has chosen and the encounter with Elroy that made his choice possible.

Though it may be removed in time, Visitation always ends in Magnificat.

the conversation continues . . .

Everything in this book has been intended as a conversation starter. Now comes the most important part of the conversation, as you name how Visitation is taking shape in your life. The following exercises may help you in that process.

Reflecting on Visitation

One way to write yourself into the scriptural story is to copy out all or part of Luke 1:39-55 by hand and then use your handwritten version to reflect on. Write as slowly as you can, not concerning yourself with the appearance of your work, so that the act of writing itself becomes contemplative. It's amazing how different the words look in a handwritten copy as opposed to a printed text. In the process, you may be inclined to pause, and perhaps copy one word or phrase several times, maybe even staying with that phrase for the rest of your reflection time.

As you become more familiar with the Visitation story, begin to tell it in your own words. If you have a reflection partner, you might tell each other the story. One can begin and let the other pick up the thread, going back and forth until the whole story has been told. Or one person can tell the whole story, while the other listens and responds to what is interesting, striking, confusing. Then, after a break, the second person tells the story, in her or his way. If you are reflecting alone, it might help to write the story down.

Whatever method you use, it's important to let your imagination fill in the blanks of the story. In his *Spiritual Exercises*, Ignatius of Loyola encourages those who meditate on a scriptural story to use as many senses as possible: what do you see? what do you hear people saying? are there any special odors? etc. (Of course, Jessica Powers would caution you to avoid inserting too many sweet-smelling flowers!) In this process, you may find yourself wanting to ask Mary or Elizabeth about their experience. When you do so, you may be surprised at the results. In fact, you may be able to let them tell you the story. Visitation looks quite different from each of their perspectives.[18]

As you listen to and tell the story of Mary and Elizabeth's Visitation, pause and contemplate the times when, for example, you too

- found yourself moving toward someone in spite of distance or obstacles or preconceptions, sometimes without quite knowing how you got to be on that road
- allowed your life to be disrupted in order to make room for a visitor so much more gifted than you
- were welcomed by those you hoped to serve—or were refused, ignored, rejected
- heard your name, felt yourself come alive, found your voice, knew God had touched you
- witnessed someone else being transformed, participated in some way in that transformation
- met God in opening yourself to someone else
- were afraid to let yourself be drawn into God's upside-down way of loving
- were "surprised by joy," as C. S. Lewis puts it, and needed to celebrate, to give thanks, to sing.

The purpose of such an exercise is not to analyze and judge, but rather to recognize the ways in which your life is already part of the journey, visit, song of Visitation.

It's also possible to begin from the opposite end, as it were, with what is happening in your life now, and asking,

- who are the Elizabeths in my life right now? who the Marys?
- what draws me to sing Magnificat? with whom can I sing it?
- with regard to a particular situation, what part of the Visitation story am I living?
- if I accept Mary and Elizabeth's invitation to join their dance, where might I move next?

In whatever way feels most comfortable, invite Mary and Elizabeth to respond to these questions with you.

It goes without saying that gazing at an image of Visitation, like Mary Southard's painting or the sculptural group from Marguerite Bourgeoys' church in Troyes, can move us more deeply into contemplation, and Christian artists over the centuries have given us thousands of these images. But the most beautiful ones, those that touch our lives most deeply, are those captured not in stone or on canvas, but on the faces and in the lives of the people whom God has visited and who allow let themselves to become the occasion of God's visitation to others.

A final vignette—

Canada, Guatemala, Cameroon, Honduras, France, El Salvador, Japan, United States. Sisters from all over the congregation, in Montreal for a meeting, gather for Eucharist. It's August 6, feast of the Transfiguration, anniversary of the U.S. bombing of Hiroshima. The mother of one sister in the room died there that day.

After communion, the briefest of rituals: each American goes to a sister from Japan, bows, gives her a red rose. What happens next hasn't been planned: every Japanese woman embraces her sister from the U.S., and that gesture goes on and on through the whole room, forgiveness asked and the blessing of peace given, some words, many tears.

Visitation.

Amen. May it be so.

Notes

1. The epigraph is taken from "Mission Song" by Kathleen Deignan, recorded on *Visitation: Songs of the Congregation of Notre Dame* (Schola Ministries, 2000). Available through www.scholaministries.org My songs "Visitation" and "Magnificat" that precede chapters 3 and 4 can be found on the same recording.

2. The best source for learning more about Marguerite Bourgeoys is Patricia Simpson's thorough two-volume biography, *Marguerite Bourgeoys and Montreal, 1640-1665* and *Marguerite Bourgeoys and the Congregation of Notre Dame, 1665-1700* (McGill-Queens University Press, 1997, 2005). Simone Poissant offers a briefer biography in *Marguerite Bourgeoys, 1620-1700* (Editions Bellarmin, 1982). My dissertation, *Apostolic Religious Life for Women: Marguerite Bourgeoys's Experiment in Ville-Marie* (Yale, 1991), treats the origins of the Congregation from historical and theological perspectives, and the last chapter explores Visitation spirituality. Information about Marguerite Bourgeoys is also available at the Congregation de Notre-Dame website www.cnd-m.com.

3. *Selected poetry of Jessica Powers*, edited by Regina Siegfried and Robert F. Morneau (Sheed & Ward, 1989), 67.

4. John S. Dunne describes the process of passing over in many of his writings, notably *The Way of All the Earth: Experiments in Truth and Religion* (Macmillan, 1972).

5. *The Jerusalem Bible* (Doubleday, 1966).

6. The quotation is taken from Pensée 46 in Pierre Teilhard de Chardin's *Hymn of the Universe*, translated by Simon Bartholomew (Harper & Row, 1965). There are numerous English translations of Martin Buber's *I and Thou*, including one by Walter Kaufmann (New York: Scribner, 1970).

7. Marty Haugen, "Gather Us In" in *Gather Comprehensive* (GIA, 1994), 744.

8. From *Where Do We Go from Here: Chaos or Community*, in *A Testament of Hope: The Essential Writings of Martin Luther King* (Harper & Row, 1986), 582.

9. A good introduction to Gandhi's writing is *Mohandas Gandhi: Essential Writings*, edited by John Dear (Maryknoll, NY : Orbis Books, 2002).

10. John Paul II's address to "Global Forum" is available at www.zenit.org/article-81?l=english Accessed 07/02/09.

11. Tim O'Brien, *The Things They Carried* (Houghton Mifflin, 1990), 52-54.

12. In *Mary of Nazareth, Prophet of Peace* (Ave Maria Press, 2003), John Dear shows how the three basic movements of the spiritual life, which he names contemplative nonviolence, active nonviolence, and prophetic nonviolence, are revealed in Mary's Annunciation, Visitation, and Magnificat.

13. This prayer, originally written by Kenneth Untener, has been reproduced widely. http://www.nationalcatholicreporter.org/peace/pfg032804.htm Accessed 07/02/09.

14. Information about the Nonviolent Peaceforce is available at their website www.nonviolentpeaceforce.org

15. In *Reaching Out: The Three Movements of the Spiritual Life* (Doubleday, 1975), Henri Nouwen identifies the second of those movements as from hostility to hospitality and illustrates how that movement can effect the teacher-student relationship.

16. Parker J. Palmer describes subject-centered education in *To Know as We Are Known: Education as a Spiritual Journey* (HarperSanFrancisco, 1993).

17. O'Brien, 52, 58.

18. Two sources that can stimulate your imagination and prayer are Elizabeth A. Johnson's *Dangerous Memories: A Mosaic of Mary in Scripture* (Continuum, 2005), which includes a meditation on the Visitation: "Joy in the Revolution of God" and Ann Johnson's *Miryam of Nazareth: Woman of Strength and Wisdom* (Ave Maria Press, 2005), the best known of several books in which Johnson imagines the kind of Magnificat Mary might sing in various situations.

Additional copies may be ordered from:

Congregation of Notre Dame
1212 Linden Street
Scranton PA 18510

mfoley@cnd-m.org